INDEX PAGE

Page 1-4	Seasonal Garden Planners
Page 5-10	Garden Shopping Lists
Page 11- 14	Garden Plot Plan & Notes
Page 15- 38	Monthly Garden Chores
Page 39- 74	Plant Profile
Page 75-94	Pest & Problems
Page 95- 104	Climate Changes Record Sheets
Pages 105-114	Notes Pages

By Divine Stationaries

PLANT NAME	JANUARY	FEBRUARY	MARCH	APRIL	MAY	JUNE	JULY	AUGUST	SEPTEMBER	OCTOBER	NOVEMBER	DECEMBER

PLANT NAME	JANUARY	FEBRUARY	MARCH	APRIL	MAY	JUNE	JULY	AUGUST	SEPTEMBER	OCTOBER	NOVEMBER	DECEMBER

PLANT NAME	JANUARY	FEBRUARY	MARCH	APRIL	MAY	JUNE	JULY	AUGUST	SEPTEMBER	OCTOBER	NOVEMBER	DECEMBER

PLANT NAME	JANUARY	FEBRUARY	MARCH	APRIL	MAY	JUNE	JULY	AUGUST	SEPTEMBER	OCTOBER	NOVEMBER	DECEMBER

SHOPPING LIST

SHOPPING LIST

SHOPPING LIST

SHOPPING LIST

SHOPPING LIST

SHOPPING LIST

GARDEN PLOT PLAN

NOTES

GARDEN PLOT PLAN

NOTES

MONTHLY GARDEN CHORES

JANUARY

MONTHLY GARDEN CHORES

FEBUARY

MONTHLY GARDEN CHORES

MARCH

MONTHLY GARDEN CHORES

APRIL

MONTHLY GARDEN CHORES

MAY

MONTHLY GARDEN CHORES

JUNE

MONTHLY GARDEN CHORES

JULY

MONTHLY GARDEN CHORES

AUGUST

MONTHLY GARDEN CHORES

SEPTEMBER

MONTHLY GARDEN CHORES

OCTOBER

MONTHLY GARDEN CHORES

NOVEMBER

MONTHLY GARDEN CHORES

DECEMBER

MONTHLY GARDEN CHORES

JANUARY

MONTHLY GARDEN CHORES

FEBUARY

MONTHLY GARDEN CHORES

MARCH

MONTHLY GARDEN CHORES

APRIL

MONTHLY GARDEN CHORES

MAY

MONTHLY GARDEN CHORES

JUNE

MONTHLY GARDEN CHORES

JULY

MONTHLY GARDEN CHORES

AUGUST

MONTHLY GARDEN CHORES

SEPTEMBER

MONTHLY GARDEN CHORES

OCTOBER

MONTHLY GARDEN CHORES

NOVEMBER

MONTHLY GARDEN CHORES

DECEMBER

PLANT PROFILE

PLANT:		DESCRIPTION:	

DATE PLANTED	QUANTITY PLANTED	CARE INSTRUCTIONS	KNOWN PROBLEMS

PROJECTED HEIGHT	PROJECTED LENGHT

HOW TO HARVEST	AMOUNT HARVESTED

NOTES/ PICTURES

PLANT PROFILE

PLANT:		DESCRIPTION:	

DATE PLANTED	QUANTITY PLANTED	CARE INSTRUCTIONS	KNOWN PROBLEMS

PROJECTED HEIGHT	PROJECTED LENGHT

HOW TO HARVEST	AMOUNT HARVESTED

NOTES/ PICTURES

PLANT PROFILE

PLANT:		DESCRIPTION:	

DATE PLANTED	QUANTITY PLANTED	CARE INSTRUCTIONS	KNOWN PROBLEMS

PROJECTED HEIGHT	PROJECTED LENGHT

HOW TO HARVEST	AMOUNT HARVESTED

NOTES/ PICTURES

PLANT PROFILE

PLANT:		DESCRIPTION:	

DATE PLANTED	QUANTITY PLANTED	CARE INSTRUCTIONS	KNOWN PROBLEMS

PROJECTED HEIGHT	PROJECTED LENGHT

HOW TO HARVEST	AMOUNT HARVESTED

NOTES/ PICTURES

PLANT PROFILE

PLANT:		DESCRIPTION:	

DATE PLANTED	QUANTITY PLANTED	CARE INSTRUCTIONS	KNOWN PROBLEMS

PROJECTED HEIGHT	PROJECTED LENGHT

HOW TO HARVEST	AMOUNT HARVESTED

NOTES/ PICTURES

PLANT PROFILE

PLANT:		DESCRIPTION:	

DATE PLANTED	QUANTITY PLANTED	CARE INSTRUCTIONS	KNOWN PROBLEMS

PROJECTED HEIGHT	PROJECTED LENGHT

HOW TO HARVEST	AMOUNT HARVESTED

NOTES/ PICTURES

PLANT PROFILE

PLANT:		DESCRIPTION:	

DATE PLANTED	QUANTITY PLANTED	CARE INSTRUCTIONS	KNOWN PROBLEMS

PROJECTED HEIGHT	PROJECTED LENGHT

HOW TO HARVEST	AMOUNT HARVESTED

NOTES/ PICTURES

PLANT PROFILE

PLANT:		DESCRIPTION:	

DATE PLANTED	QUANTITY PLANTED	CARE INSTRUCTIONS	KNOWN PROBLEMS

PROJECTED HEIGHT	PROJECTED LENGHT

HOW TO HARVEST	AMOUNT HARVESTED

NOTES/ PICTURES

PLANT PROFILE

PLANT:		DESCRIPTION:	

DATE PLANTED	QUANTITY PLANTED	CARE INSTRUCTIONS	KNOWN PROBLEMS

PROJECTED HEIGHT	PROJECTED LENGHT

HOW TO HARVEST	AMOUNT HARVESTED

NOTES/ PICTURES

PLANT PROFILE

PLANT:		DESCRIPTION:	

DATE PLANTED	QUANTITY PLANTED	CARE INSTRUCTIONS	KNOWN PROBLEMS

PROJECTED HEIGHT	PROJECTED LENGHT

HOW TO HARVEST	AMOUNT HARVESTED

NOTES/ PICTURES

PLANT PROFILE

PLANT:		DESCRIPTION:	

DATE PLANTED	QUANTITY PLANTED	CARE INSTRUCTIONS	KNOWN PROBLEMS

PROJECTED HEIGHT	PROJECTED LENGHT

HOW TO HARVEST	AMOUNT HARVESTED

NOTES/ PICTURES

PLANT PROFILE

PLANT:		DESCRIPTION:	

DATE PLANTED	QUANTITY PLANTED	CARE INSTRUCTIONS	KNOWN PROBLEMS

PROJECTED HEIGHT	PROJECTED LENGHT

HOW TO HARVEST	AMOUNT HARVESTED

NOTES/ PICTURES

PLANT PROFILE

PLANT:		DESCRIPTION:	

DATE PLANTED	QUANTITY PLANTED	CARE INSTRUCTIONS	KNOWN PROBLEMS

PROJECTED HEIGHT	PROJECTED LENGHT

HOW TO HARVEST	AMOUNT HARVESTED

NOTES/ PICTURES

PLANT PROFILE

PLANT:		DESCRIPTION:	

DATE PLANTED	QUANTITY PLANTED	CARE INSTRUCTIONS	KNOWN PROBLEMS

PROJECTED HEIGHT	PROJECTED LENGHT

HOW TO HARVEST	AMOUNT HARVESTED

NOTES/ PICTURES

PLANT PROFILE

PLANT:		DESCRIPTION:	

DATE PLANTED	QUANTITY PLANTED	CARE INSTRUCTIONS	KNOWN PROBLEMS

PROJECTED HEIGHT	PROJECTED LENGHT

HOW TO HARVEST	AMOUNT HARVESTED

NOTES/ PICTURES

PLANT PROFILE

PLANT:		DESCRIPTION:	

DATE PLANTED	QUANTITY PLANTED	CARE INSTRUCTIONS	KNOWN PROBLEMS

PROJECTED HEIGHT	PROJECTED LENGHT

HOW TO HARVEST	AMOUNT HARVESTED

NOTES/ PICTURES

PLANT PROFILE

PLANT:		DESCRIPTION:	

DATE PLANTED	QUANTITY PLANTED	CARE INSTRUCTIONS	KNOWN PROBLEMS

PROJECTED HEIGHT	PROJECTED LENGHT

HOW TO HARVEST	AMOUNT HARVESTED

NOTES/ PICTURES

PLANT PROFILE

PLANT:		DESCRIPTION:	

DATE PLANTED	QUANTITY PLANTED	CARE INSTRUCTIONS	KNOWN PROBLEMS

PROJECTED HEIGHT	PROJECTED LENGHT

HOW TO HARVEST	AMOUNT HARVESTED

NOTES/ PICTURES

PLANT PROFILE

PLANT:		DESCRIPTION:	

DATE PLANTED	QUANTITY PLANTED	CARE INSTRUCTIONS	KNOWN PROBLEMS

PROJECTED HEIGHT	PROJECTED LENGHT

HOW TO HARVEST	AMOUNT HARVESTED

NOTES/ PICTURES

PLANT PROFILE

PLANT:		DESCRIPTION:	

DATE PLANTED	QUANTITY PLANTED	CARE INSTRUCTIONS	KNOWN PROBLEMS

PROJECTED HEIGHT	PROJECTED LENGHT

HOW TO HARVEST	AMOUNT HARVESTED

NOTES/ PICTURES

PLANT PROFILE

| PLANT: | | DESCRIPTION: | |

DATE PLANTED	QUANTITY PLANTED	CARE INSTRUCTIONS	KNOWN PROBLEMS

PROJECTED HEIGHT	PROJECTED LENGHT

HOW TO HARVEST	AMOUNT HARVESTED

NOTES/ PICTURES

PLANT PROFILE

PLANT:		DESCRIPTION:	

DATE PLANTED	QUANTITY PLANTED	CARE INSTRUCTIONS	KNOWN PROBLEMS

PROJECTED HEIGHT	PROJECTED LENGHT

HOW TO HARVEST	AMOUNT HARVESTED

NOTES/ PICTURES

PLANT PROFILE

PLANT:		DESCRIPTION:	

DATE PLANTED	QUANTITY PLANTED	CARE INSTRUCTIONS	KNOWN PROBLEMS

PROJECTED HEIGHT	PROJECTED LENGHT

HOW TO HARVEST	AMOUNT HARVESTED

NOTES/ PICTURES

PLANT PROFILE

PLANT:		DESCRIPTION:	

DATE PLANTED	QUANTITY PLANTED	CARE INSTRUCTIONS	KNOWN PROBLEMS

PROJECTED HEIGHT	PROJECTED LENGHT

HOW TO HARVEST	AMOUNT HARVESTED

NOTES/ PICTURES

PLANT PROFILE

| PLANT: | | DESCRIPTION: | |
|---|---|---|---|</p>

DATE PLANTED	QUANTITY PLANTED	CARE INSTRUCTIONS	KNOWN PROBLEMS

PROJECTED HEIGHT	PROJECTED LENGHT

HOW TO HARVEST	AMOUNT HARVESTED

NOTES/ PICTURES

PLANT PROFILE

PLANT:	DESCRIPTION:

DATE PLANTED	QUANTITY PLANTED	CARE INSTRUCTIONS	KNOWN PROBLEMS

PROJECTED HEIGHT	PROJECTED LENGHT

HOW TO HARVEST	AMOUNT HARVESTED

NOTES/ PICTURES

PLANT PROFILE

PLANT:		DESCRIPTION:	

DATE PLANTED	QUANTITY PLANTED	CARE INSTRUCTIONS	KNOWN PROBLEMS

PROJECTED HEIGHT	PROJECTED LENGHT

HOW TO HARVEST	AMOUNT HARVESTED

NOTES/ PICTURES

PLANT PROFILE

PLANT:		DESCRIPTION:	

DATE PLANTED	QUANTITY PLANTED	CARE INSTRUCTIONS	KNOWN PROBLEMS

PROJECTED HEIGHT	PROJECTED LENGHT

HOW TO HARVEST	AMOUNT HARVESTED

NOTES/ PICTURES

PLANT PROFILE

PLANT:		DESCRIPTION:	

DATE PLANTED	QUANTITY PLANTED	CARE INSTRUCTIONS	KNOWN PROBLEMS

PROJECTED HEIGHT	PROJECTED LENGHT

HOW TO HARVEST	AMOUNT HARVESTED

NOTES/ PICTURES

PLANT PROFILE

PLANT:		DESCRIPTION:	

DATE PLANTED	QUANTITY PLANTED	CARE INSTRUCTIONS	KNOWN PROBLEMS

PROJECTED HEIGHT	PROJECTED LENGHT

HOW TO HARVEST	AMOUNT HARVESTED

NOTES/ PICTURES

PLANT PROFILE

PLANT:		DESCRIPTION:	

DATE PLANTED	QUANTITY PLANTED	CARE INSTRUCTIONS	KNOWN PROBLEMS

PROJECTED HEIGHT	PROJECTED LENGHT

HOW TO HARVEST	AMOUNT HARVESTED

NOTES/ PICTURES

PLANT PROFILE

PLANT:		DESCRIPTION:	

DATE PLANTED	QUANTITY PLANTED	CARE INSTRUCTIONS	KNOWN PROBLEMS

PROJECTED HEIGHT	PROJECTED LENGHT

HOW TO HARVEST	AMOUNT HARVESTED

NOTES/ PICTURES

PLANT PROFILE

PLANT:		DESCRIPTION:	

DATE PLANTED	QUANTITY PLANTED	CARE INSTRUCTIONS	KNOWN PROBLEMS

PROJECTED HEIGHT	PROJECTED LENGHT

HOW TO HARVEST	AMOUNT HARVESTED

NOTES/ PICTURES

PLANT PROFILE

PLANT:		DESCRIPTION:	

DATE PLANTED	QUANTITY PLANTED	CARE INSTRUCTIONS	KNOWN PROBLEMS

PROJECTED HEIGHT	PROJECTED LENGHT

HOW TO HARVEST	AMOUNT HARVESTED

NOTES/ PICTURES

PLANT PROFILE

PLANT:		DESCRIPTION:	

DATE PLANTED	QUANTITY PLANTED	CARE INSTRUCTIONS	KNOWN PROBLEMS

PROJECTED HEIGHT	PROJECTED LENGHT

HOW TO HARVEST	AMOUNT HARVESTED

NOTES/ PICTURES

PLANT PROFILE

PLANT:		DESCRIPTION:	

DATE PLANTED	QUANTITY PLANTED	CARE INSTRUCTIONS	KNOWN PROBLEMS

PROJECTED HEIGHT	PROJECTED LENGHT

HOW TO HARVEST	AMOUNT HARVESTED

NOTES/ PICTURES

PESTS & PROBLEMS

DATE	PLANT	PROBLEM	TREATMENT	EFFECTIVE?

PESTS & PROBLEMS

NOTES

PESTS & PROBLEMS

DATE	PLANT	PROBLEM	TREATMENT	EFFECTIVE?

PESTS & PROBLEMS

NOTES

PESTS & PROBLEMS

DATE	PLANT	PROBLEM	TREATMENT	EFFECTIVE?

PESTS & PROBLEMS

NOTES

PESTS & PROBLEMS

DATE	PLANT	PROBLEM	TREATMENT	EFFECTIVE?

PESTS & PROBLEMS

NOTES

PESTS & PROBLEMS

DATE	PLANT	PROBLEM	TREATMENT	EFFECTIVE?

PESTS & PROBLEMS

NOTES

PESTS & PROBLEMS

DATE	PLANT	PROBLEM	TREATMENT	EFFECTIVE?

PESTS & PROBLEMS

NOTES

PESTS & PROBLEMS

DATE	PLANT	PROBLEM	TREATMENT	EFFECTIVE?

PESTS & PROBLEMS

NOTES

PESTS & PROBLEMS

DATE	PLANT	PROBLEM	TREATMENT	EFFECTIVE?

PESTS & PROBLEMS

NOTES

PESTS & PROBLEMS

DATE	PLANT	PROBLEM	TREATMENT	EFFECTIVE?

PESTS & PROBLEMS

NOTES

PESTS & PROBLEMS

DATE	PLANT	PROBLEM	TREATMENT	EFFECTIVE?

PESTS & PROBLEMS

NOTES

CLIMATE DATA WORTH NOTING

DATE:_____

DATE:_____

DATE:_____

DATE:_____

DATE:_____

DATE:_____

DATE:_____

DATE:_____

DATE:_____

DATE:_____

DATE:_____

DATE:_____

DATE:_____

DATE:_____

DATE:_____

DATE:_____

DATE:_____

CLIMATE DATA WORTH NOTING

DATE:_____

DATE:_____

DATE:_____

DATE:_____

DATE:_____

DATE:_____

DATE:_____

DATE:_____

DATE:_____

DATE:_____

DATE:_____

DATE:_____

DATE:_____

DATE:_____

DATE:_____

DATE:_____

DATE:_____

DATE:_____

CLIMATE DATA WORTH NOTING

DATE:_____

DATE:_____

DATE:_____

DATE:_____

DATE:_____

DATE:_____

DATE:_____

DATE:_____

DATE:_____

DATE:_____

DATE:_____

DATE:_____

DATE:_____

DATE:_____

DATE:_____

DATE:_____

DATE:_____

DATE:_____

CLIMATE DATA WORTH NOTING

DATE:_____

DATE:_____

DATE:_____

DATE:_____

DATE:_____

DATE:_____

DATE:_____

DATE:_____

DATE:_____

DATE:_____

DATE:_____

DATE:_____

DATE:_____

DATE:_____

DATE:_____

DATE:_____

DATE:_____

DATE:_____

DATE:_____

CLIMATE DATA WORTH NOTING

DATE:_____

DATE:_____

DATE:_____

DATE:_____

DATE:_____

DATE:_____

DATE:_____

DATE:_____

DATE:_____

DATE:_____

DATE:_____

DATE:_____

DATE:_____

DATE:_____

DATE:_____

DATE:_____

DATE:_____

CLIMATE DATA WORTH NOTING

DATE:_____

DATE:_____

DATE:_____

DATE:_____

DATE:_____

DATE:_____

DATE:_____

DATE:_____

DATE:_____

DATE:_____

DATE:_____

DATE:_____

DATE:_____

DATE:_____

DATE:_____

DATE:_____

DATE:_____

CLIMATE DATA WORTH NOTING

DATE:_____

DATE:_____

DATE:_____

DATE:_____

DATE:_____

DATE:_____

DATE:_____

DATE:_____

DATE:_____

DATE:_____

DATE:_____

DATE:_____

DATE:_____

DATE:_____

DATE:_____

DATE:_____

DATE:_____

DATE:_____

CLIMATE DATA WORTH NOTING

DATE:_____

DATE:_____

DATE:_____

DATE:_____

DATE:_____

DATE:_____

DATE:_____

DATE:_____

DATE:_____

DATE:_____

DATE:_____

DATE:_____

DATE:_____

DATE:_____

DATE:_____

DATE:_____

DATE:_____

DATE:_____

CLIMATE DATA WORTH NOTING

DATE:_____

DATE:_____

DATE:_____

DATE:_____

DATE:_____

DATE:_____

DATE:_____

DATE:_____

DATE:_____

DATE:_____

DATE:_____

DATE:_____

DATE:_____

DATE:_____

DATE:_____

DATE:_____

DATE:_____

CLIMATE DATA WORTH NOTING

DATE:_____

DATE:_____

DATE:_____

DATE:_____

DATE:_____

DATE:_____

DATE:_____

DATE:_____

DATE:_____

DATE:_____

DATE:_____

DATE:_____

DATE:_____

DATE:_____

DATE:_____

DATE:_____

DATE:_____

DATE:_____

NOTES

NOTES

NOTES

NOTES

NOTES

NOTES

NOTES

NOTES

NOTES

NOTES

Made in the USA
San Bernardino, CA
26 November 2018